Chromebook

GW00994575

Guide for Chrome OS Apps, Tips & Tricks!

By Shelby Johnson

Disclaimer:

This eBook is an unofficial guide and general companion manual for Google Chromebook, and it should not be considered a replacement for any instructions, documentation or other information provided with the Chromebook device or by Google on their associated websites. The information in this guide is meant as recommendations and suggestions, but the author bears no responsibility for any issues arising from improper use of the devices mentioned within. The owner of the device is responsible for taking all necessary precautions and measures with their Chromebook.

Images and screenshots were acquired from Google Chromebook setup pages, Chrome browser, Amazon, or taken by the author, and they imply no affiliation with Google or the Chromebook device, or Amazon.

Contents

—

Introduction

If you've got a Chromebook, you just may be part of the future of computing as these particular devices continue to surge in popularity. To date, there have been at least 17 Chromebook models released, ranging back to 2010-2011 with the Google Cr-48 and the Samsung Series 5.

Since then, even more models have been produced with better features such as more battery life, faster processors, touchscreens, and better screen resolutions. These have included models created by popular brands such as HP, Samsung, Acer, Dell, Google and Toshiba.

Chromebooks tend to be lightweight notebook-style computers that have screen displays that vary in size from 11 to 14-inches. For the most part, these devices all rely on the same overall Chrome OS (operating system) and use web browser-integrated features, although the specs and features may differ by brand.

This general guide has been tested with several of the newer models available such as the Acer C720P touchscreen and the Samsung Chromebook 2, and should also be helpful for those with somewhat older models of the Chromebook. The guide isn't intended to replace brand-specific user guides, but rather to provide tips, tricks and other helpful info for Chromebooks. It is always important to consult specific documents or instructions that were included with each specific model as well, as this guide is not meant to replace those in any way, shape or form.

Basic Specs & Inputs/Outputs for Chromebooks

Chromebooks are designed to go anywhere, and deliver an exciting resolution once the top is opened to unveil the greatness of the built-in Chrome OS. All Chromebook models are different, but some of the basic specs that these powerful laptops commonly include might be:

- Dimensions: 7.68 x 11.69 x 0.69 Inches or bigger
- Weight: 2.3 Pounds or more
- Screen Size: 11.6 Inches or larger
- Screen Resolution: 1366 x 768
- Processor: 1.4 GHz or more Intel, or other brand
- RAM: at least 2GB DDR3L SDRAM
- Hard Drive: at least 16GB Solid State Drive (SSD)

- Ports: Two USB ports, HDMI output on some models, One MicroUSB for 15.75W Charging & SlimPort Video Output on some models
- Battery Life: Six to Eight Hours (based on model)
- Combined Headphone/Microphone Jack
- Digitally-tuned Speakers with Sound Directed Up, Through the Keyboard
- Dual-band Wi-Fi
- Bluetooth 4.0

In addition to its savvy processing capabilities, and magnificently petite design, the complementary features include a well-built chassis that provides optimal strength, a silent, fan-less design and no visible screws, vents or speakers providing a superior, sleek design at your fingertips.

Some of the newer models included touchscreen functionality, such as the Acer C720P and the Lenovo N20p, which will provide even more of a notebook/tablet feeling for owners of these nifty devices.

Keyboard Layout

Most Chromebooks feature a different keyboard layout than a typical laptop or desktop computer. While all the letters and number keys are available, as well as popular keys such as backspace, enter/return and space bar, there are no dedicated delete or caps lock keys on board.

The Chromebook keyboard does not have any F keys (function keys) located on the top. Instead, there are various images on the keys on the keyboard's top row, which represent different functions. The following screenshot shows exactly what each key represents.

Key	Function
←	Go to the previous page in your browser history (F1)
→	Go to the next page in your browser history (F2)
⟳	Reload your current page (F3)
▱	Enter Immersive mode, which hides the tabs and launcher (F4)
▭	Enter Overview mode, which shows all windows (F5)
◌	Decrease screen brightness (F6)
✳	Increase screen brightness (F7)
◀×	Mute (F8)
◀−	Decrease the volume (F9)
◀+	Increase the volume (F10)

For a description of Delete and Caps Lock keyboard functions, check out this section of the book. Also, you can find more information about these keys as well as other keys and keyboard shortcuts here: https://support.google.com/chromebook/answer/1047364?hl=en.

☐

Chrome OS

Chrome is an operating system (OS) designed and implemented by Google. It is a web browser-based OS that works primarily with web applications, and dedicates its design success to a minimalist approach to user friendliness. Although nearly the entirety of the operating system is dedicated to Google Chrome, there is also a media player and file manager that comprises its overall capabilities and existence. The goal of Chrome OS is to provide a premier option for those who spend most of their computer time on the web and want a quick way to get booted up with their device.

Since Chrome OS is mostly an online operating system based on the Chrome web browser, Chromebooks don't have the ability to install programs like a desktop or traditional laptop does. That means programs like MS Office, Skype and Adobe Photoshop are out of play. In addition, there is no Java functionality with the Chrome OS, which takes away the ability to play certain games or use certain chats online, among other things. (There is a workaround discussed later in this guide for changing the OS).

However, the Chrome OS provides a great lightweight experience for those who want a simplistic device, minus the complications of a file system, viruses and other hassles that might accompany traditional computers.

Cloud-based Storage & Browser-based apps

With Google Chrome comes the brilliance of Google Drive, which provides 15 GBs of free cloud storage space that enables users to enjoy a cloud-based backup system for their files. This means that individuals with a Chrome account can access their saved and shared documents from any Internet connection simply by logging in.

Google Drive provides more than storage space, but also the ability to share documents in a public or private forum, simply by providing the audience with a web link to the document. There is no software to download, and no tricky conversion processes necessary. The only thing the viewer has to do is click the link and view the available files created for their edification.

What's more is that Google Drive provides access to browser-based apps that are designed by third parties, in addition to the "software" the Drive provides as Google Docs, which is a document app, Google Sheets, which is a spreadsheet app, and Google Slides, which performs much like a PowerPoint presentation.

It addition, the app Quickoffice allows users to open Microsoft Word files, including documents, spreadsheets, and slide shows, while providing the ability to manipulate the files, sign them, save them and return them to their rightful owner.

Google also has forms that allow users to create surveys, design invitations, and create to do lists and reoccurring daily activities, all from anywhere. With over 100 Drive apps, photos, videos, presentations and file management can be created, manipulated, saved, signed and delivered all from the moment your Google Drive account is opened.

Google Drive can support the following files:

- Google Docs

- Google Sheets
- Google Slides
- Google Forms
- Google Drawings
- Image files (.JPEG, .PNG, .GIF, .TIFF, .BMP)
- Video files (WebM, .MPEG4, .3GPP, .MOV, .AVI, .MPEGPS, .WMV, .FLV, .OGG)
- Text files (.TXT)
- Markup/Code (.CSS, .HTML, .PHP, .C, .CPP, .H, .HPP, .JS)
- Microsoft Word (.DOC and .DOCX)
- Microsoft Excel (.XLS and .XLSX)
- Microsoft PowerPoint (.PPT and .PPTX)
- Adobe Portable Document Format (.PDF)
- Apple Pages (.PAGES)
- Adobe Illustrator (.AI)
- Adobe Photoshop (.PSD)
- Autodesk AutoCad (.DXF)
- Scalable Vector Graphics (.SVG)
- PostScript (.EPS, .PS)
- Fonts (.TTF, .OTF)
- XML Paper Specification (.XPS)
- Archive file types (.ZIP and .RAR)
- .MTS Files

You can easily start your collection today, and enjoy the 15 free GB of storage by logging into your Google account from your Chromebook. Should you need extra storage space, Google will supply larger increments at a cost. Users can receive 100GB of storage for $1.99 per month or 1TB for $9.99 per month. Google Drive is built into Chromebooks, which means all files and photos are automatically backed up once the laptop is set up. Also, with most new Chromebook models, 100GB of storage comes free for two years so there is no need to upgrade.

Getting Started/Initial Setup

Google provides the world with a wickedly easy setup approach with everything they produce. This is the allure of their technological feats: It will be easy to access, use and share with others. Getting started with your Chromebook will be a simple process. Once you turn the Chromebook on, you will be ready to connect to a whole new world.

First you will need to create a Google account, which can include Gmail, Google Drive, Play, Maps, Plus, YouTube, Chrome and file storage access, all using a single username and password. Again, simplicity takes center stage.

Simply logon to https://accounts.google.com/SignUp?service=mail and fill out the online form, which simply asks for your name, the creation of a username and password, birthday, gender, phone number and a current email address to confirm the activation of this account. Lastly, enter your location and a security code that appears onscreen to prove that you are not a robot. It is that easy!

Keep in mind that if you sign up for a Gmail account, you will automatically receive access to a Google Account, using the same information. However, it is not necessary to have Gmail account to access all things Google. The choice is yours completely.

The next steps will entail applying your personal preferences to your account. These items can be changed at any time, and are completely up to your personal preference. There is no need to overthink the process, as Google will help guide you through the available options and what they mean to your personal use.

Once you have created an account, you will be connected to each of the features Google has to offer automatically and can begin using each of the web-based apps as you see fit!

Chromebook Features

Now that your account is up and running, it is time to put the Chromebook to use for you! Let's take a look at the Chrome OS layout, settings and applications. With these Chrome OS delivers premier access to productivity and communicative wherewithal, so you can stay in touch with others, personally and professionally, without stepping out from behind your Chromebook.

Chrome OS Screen Layout

You'll notice that the screen simply has a wallpaper backdrop image, and then several icons or panels along the lower edge of the display.

An apps menu square icon is located in the lower left corner of your screen. This icon is a blue square with nine smaller white squares in it (as seen in the image). You can click on this icon to bring up a menu of all of your installed apps, and to quickly perform a web search for anything you need to find by using the search box. Next to the apps menu icon you may also see commonly used apps such as Chrome, Gmail, Google search, Docs, YouTube and more.

Quick tip: When you pull up your apps menu, you can right-click on any app to "Pin to shelf." This will place it among the apps at the bottom of your screen. You can also right-click on any app and choose "Uninstall" should you want to remove it from your Chromebook.

An information and settings bar is located in the lower right corner of your screen. You'll see the current time, your network and Bluetooth connections and a small image resembling your Google account photo here. You can click on this bar to bring up quick settings for your device including Network connection, battery power and your Google account (or Guest status). You can also use this area to log out of your account or power down your Chromebook. By clicking on "Settings" you'll bring up even more settings you can adjust for your Chrome OS that are discussed in the next section.

Modifying Layout

Right-click on your Chromebook screen (when the Wallpaper is showing) to bring up three different options.

Autohide shelf - Hides the lower shelf that includes your apps and the information settings bars described above. To reveal it again, simply move your cursor to the bottom of the screen.

Shelf position - You can also change the position of this lower shelf so that it is on the right or left side of your screen, rather than the bottom area.

Set wallpaper - One other option you'll get is that you can "Set wallpaper" to change the image that is displayed as your backdrop.

Chrome OS Settings

By clicking on the lower right hand corner bar on your Chromebook display (where the time and your Google account photo is) you can access the Chrome OS "Settings." Here's a brief overview of what can be done with these various aspects of your device.

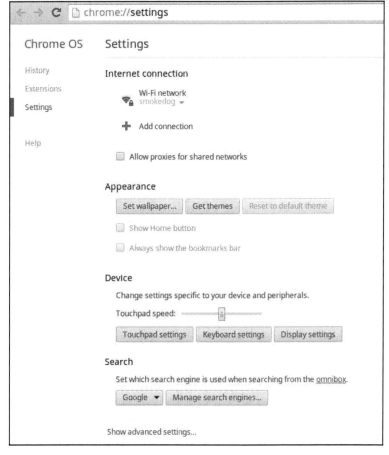

- **Internet connection** – use this to manage your Wi-Fi, 3G/4G and other connections. You can also set up proxies for shared networks here.

- **Appearance** – If you want to customize the look of your Chromebook's Wallpaper, this is the place to do it. You can also get other themes to use here, or restore to the original default theme your Chromebook originally had.
- **Device** – Use these settings to fine-tune your Touchpad, Keyboard and Display.
- **Search** – With this, you can change your custom search engine for the omnibox. The omnibox is the search box you'll see above all your apps on the apps menu (found by clicking lower-left apps icon which is nine small squares together).
- **Users** – If you're logged into a Google account on your Chromebook, you'll see that account here. You can easily manage synced data on Google Dashboard, set up advanced sync settings or manage other accounts (users) here.

Advanced settings

- There may be a link which you can click on to reveal your Chrome OS "Advanced Settings." This is where you can get into even more aspects of your Chrome OS and Chromebook. These include:
- **Date and time settings** - For changing the date and/or time manually, as well as use a 24-hour clock.
- **Privacy settings for browsing** – For maintaining your privacy and protection while browsing the Internet on your device.
- **Bluetooth settings** – Use this to enable/disable Bluetooth on your Chromebook, to add Bluetooth devices and to see which devices are currently connected.
- **Passwords and form settings** – Use these settings to make it easier to fill out your info on webforms, or for the browser to offer to save passwords on websites you log into, for use the next time you visit them.

- **Web content** - Use these settings to adjust web content display aspects such as font size, type and page zoom percentage)
- **Languages** – You can change your Chromebook's language and language input settings here. Also you can enable or disable whether Chrome offers to translate webpages for you that are in different languages.
- **Downloads location and preferences** – For choosing where to store any files you might download on your Chromebook (you can also disable Google Drive on your device here).
- **HTTPS/SSL** – A complex setting for managing server certificates that your browser may use.
- **Google Cloud Print settings** – Used for adding and managing your various connected printers on Google Cloud.
- **On startup** - This can set how your Chrome browser looks when you first open it. You can specify whether you want a specific page, just a new tab page or to continue where you left off last time.
- **Accessibility settings** - Change various aspects such as making a larger mouse cursor, have spoken feedback provided, a screen magnifier, on-screen keyboard and more.
- **Powerwash** – This is an easy way to reset your Chromebook to be like new again, wiping out all user accounts on the device. It should also mostly be used in extreme cases. There is more on the Powerwash feature of Chromebook later in this guide.
- **Reset browser settings** – Use this in extreme cases for restoring your browser settings to be just as they originally were.

Using Cloud Services

With the purchase of a newer model, owners will receive 100GB of cloud storage for free for two years. That is a lot of space! Without the newest version, 15GB is readily available and is an excellent way to store anything and everything in the cloud, so it can be accessed at any time, from any device with an Internet connection.

Google Cloud allows account owners to save documents, images, videos, presentations and files of differing styles in an online access account that is protected by their servers. This means you can back up your Chromebook into the cloud space providing, of course and access the information saved from any device, anywhere, any time. Whether you are looking for items from your tablet, smartphone or even from a large desktop computer at a local library, your cloud can be accessed from anywhere there is an Internet connection. This means you will never be without all of your important items even if one of them is a picture of your beloved no matter where you are.

Google Hangouts

Google Hangouts is an instant messaging and video chat application that allows two or more people to hold conversations via text while sharing images as the conversation unfolds. Each person involved in the conversation is represented by an avatar, which can be chosen when you set up your account or one will be assigned by Google. During the conversation, this avatar will be used as a marker to indicate how far you have reached in the conversation, so the other person or people know what information has been received or read to date.

Images, text and emoticons shared during this hangout will be saved automatically to Google+. In addition to the texting form of Hangouts, there is also a video chat forum that will allow up to ten people to communicate, face to face, at one time. This allows for easy access to others to create meeting times, coordinate plans, or simply catch up on the go. This is recommended in lieu of the popular Skype application, which as of this publication, does not function on Chromebooks.

Google Docs

Google Docs allows users to create, upload and share documents from anywhere there is a web connection. Within the Google Docs app, users can create a document, presentation, spreadsheet, form or even draw. Once a file is created, it can be saved, edited or even shared by tapping the "Share" button, which will reveal a link that the user can send to the person they want to see it. This sharing process can be public or private, and the user has the ability to decide whether or not the person opening it can edit the document or not. This is great for teams who are working on a project together, as one can add their portion and share it with another, allowing them to add their portion and so on and so on.

Other files that are sent to you the user can be opened in Google Docs, even if they are a Word document or Excel spreadsheet, making it a very handy tool for those who mix business, school and pleasure from their Chromebook.

Google Play

Google Play is a digital distribution platform that allows users to download apps, music, magazines, books, movies and television programs. As an online electronics and digital media outlet, users can connect a credit card number, PayPal or their bank account to their Google Play account, and purchase apps and entertainment on the go.

Although there are a number of apps that cost money, there are others that are free and allow you to enhance your online experience by downloading them through Google Play. You can learn more on the awesome apps you can add to your device later in this guide.

Games (at Google Play)

Within Google Play, there is a segment for games, and games only! This is the perfect way to separate the business, school or personal apps from the fun of gaming. Simply tap the tab called "Games" and Google will reveal the top rated games, free games, paid games and those that appeal to you by keyword searches. For instance, if you are a fan of "bubble" games, simply type in the word "bubble" to reveal any games, free or paid, that has the word in the description. Otherwise, check out the reviews and download the ones that appeal to you. You have plenty of space on your Chromebook, so use it!

Not only will you discover great games, but also you can play with friends online by joining multiplayer games and track your (and everyone else's) achievements.

Working Offline (Gmail, Google Docs)

Sometimes Wi-Fi may be hard to come by, even if it seems like it is accessible everywhere from your doctor's office to your favorite coffee shop. When you cannot come by the ever-valuable hotspot, it is possible to work in Gmail and Google Docs while offline.

First, you must install the Gmail Offline app in Chrome using a live Internet connection and allow it to download completely. While offline, you can archive, label, delete, compose emails, and much more. Once back online, all pending actions will automatically update in your Gmail.

Working offline with Google Docs is equally simple. Even without an Internet connection you can get your work completed while scratching items from your to do list simply by working offline. With this option users can organize folders, view and edit files, spreadsheets, presentations and drawings.

If you happen to be using the new Google Drive, offline access is already set up for you. If not, you can turn this incredible helpful tool by clicking "Settings" followed by "Offline" and checking the box next to the phrase "Sync your work to this computer so that you can edit offline." Google really spells it out for you, which is fantastic.

Using Chromebook for Media

What good is a laptop with the ability to enjoy all of your favorite entertainment? Chromebook has you covered, allow videos, movies and even reading to come to life like you have not seen it before!

Watching Videos or Movies

Watching videos and movies on your Chromebook is easy, and with access to all of your favorite media outlets you can easily login to your accounts and enjoy new and classic videos, movies and television shows with ease.

Netflix, Amazon Video & Google Play

If you have a Netflix, Hulu Plus or Amazon Video you can sign into your account directly from your Chrome browser and enjoy their entire libraries in brilliant color directly from your laptop. Keep in mind you will need an active Internet connection (Wi-Fi, 3G/4G) in order to stream movies to your Chromebook.

Google Play is the place to find music, movies and television shows that are available directly from the app on your desktop, pre-loaded on your Chromebook. Simply click on it, and search for the exact title, actor, musician or genre that you are looking for before streaming it directly on your screen or in your music player.

Using Kindle eBooks

When using a Chromebook, you have the option to use the Kindle Cloud Reader app, which works great for reading your current eBook online or offline. The web app allows you to do all of the things a regular Kindle would, like change fonts, save your last read page, create and edit notes and even allow you to search the material for characters, subject matter or points of interest. In addition, readers can enjoy delving into the eBook's content by tapping on a word or phrase to be examined closely (i.e., a city, character affiliation, etc.) without moving from the page you are on!

In addition to using the Kindle Cloud Reader app, you can also access the Kindle Cloud Reader on a Chrome browser tab and sign into your account to read eBooks directly from your browser.

Using Camera(s)

Google's Chromebook has a webcam, which allows you to video chat with friends and family, or sit in on a virtual meeting with ease. However, when it comes to taking a still picture, you will need to download an app that fits your liking. There is a simple camera app that will allow you to take pictures, add filters and themes. There is also Webcam Toy app that allows you to play with over 80 different effects while saving pictures to your computer or sharing them on social media.

Editing Photos and Images

The Chrome OS already has a basic image editing feature built right into it, which includes the ability to crop, brighten and rotate your photos. What about if you want to perform more advanced edits on your images though?

Since you can't install programs on a Chromebook, there's no way to use something that is on the same level as Adobe Photoshop. However, there are also multiple apps available, which serve different purposes in terms of editing images. Probably the most popular (and best) option out there currently is an app called Pixl Editor. Use this app with your Chromebook to edit and fix your photos, add effects and apply various filters. It's a great addition to your collection of apps, with more discussion on this particular app later in this guide.

Editing Video Files

Since there is no built-in video editor, the best option is to add an app called WeVideo. This app operates as a cloud based video creation tool that allows users to record video, edit on the go, and upload the completed clip to social media with ease.

With three levels of interface, novice users who have never edited video before will be completely comfortable diving into WeVideo's capabilities. With three modes, users can jump right to the platform they are comfortable with, even at an expert level, or allow their video editing knowledge to grow in stages.

WeVideo has 20 unique themes that allow videos to acquire a specific ton and texture with a single click. Professional transitions, typography, visual effects and sound tracks are all available at the tap of a finger, and allow videos to come to life, without the complexity of professional editing suites.

All you have to do is create a storyboard by arranging the clips in the order you would like for them to appear, trim them for awesome timing, apply a theme and share the results with the world!

Editing Audio or Making Music

While there isn't a built-in way to create audio files or make music, there are several apps and/or extensions that can be added to your Chrome OS browser to do so. These will be discussed a bit more in detail later in this guide. One simple app you can add to your Chrome OS is called TwistedWave. This app is free to install and by signing up for a free account you can perform more than 30 seconds of audio editing. With the editor you can cut down audio tracks, add effects and then save your work to either Google Drive or Soundcloud.

Other audio editor app tools to consider include Audiotool and AudioSauna, both of which are more for slightly more serious music makers.

Chromebook Apps

Chromebook Apps are available in the Chrome App Store, at https://chrome.google.com/webstore/. This store can be accessed exclusively online, and filtered by apps, extensions and themes. You can choose to filter these items by features including those that run offline, those that are Google designed, those that are free and those that are available for Android.

Adding & Deleting Apps

When adding apps to your Chromebook, all you have to do is click on the icon that says "Free" or lists a price for its purchase. Once you do, the system will relay that it is "Checking" before adding the app to your list. Once it is available, which will be clear through a tab that automatically opens in Chrome, simply click on the newest download to begin using it.

If you are unsatisfied with an app at any time, you can delete it from your list effortlessly. Simply right-click on the icon, select "Remove from Chrome" and confirm this removal by clicking the "Remove" when prompted. You can do this as often or as little as you would like!

Can You Install Android Apps?

Currently, Chromebook users cannot install Android Apps on their laptops. However, Google has announced at the end of June 2014 that "soon" Chromebook and Chrome OS users will, indeed, be able to install Android Apps on their devices. An actual date was not released, but with this addition to the Chromebook coming soon, it only enhances its appeal!

25 Chromebook Apps to Get You Moving

As previously mentioned in this guide, apps are generally easy to add for free (or for a cost) via the Chrome Web Store online. For those looking to really take their Chromebook device to the next level, installing some of the apps outlined below will certainly make it much more productive.

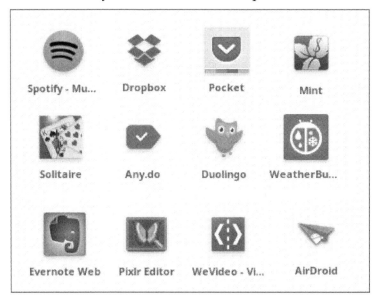

Keep in mind that some apps will indicate at Chrome Web Store that they can work offline, while others will not. There is also a way to narrow down apps at the store by clicking on the "Runs Offline" option on the left side of the screen under "Features."

Now, without further adieu, here are 25 apps definitely worth checking out and installing for your device.

Gmail Offline Beta

This is a Gmail app that was built to help provide offline access. With the app, you are able to read, reply, archive and search for mails without an Internet connection. This app would provide an excellent email-focused experience to the intended user. This app will automatically synchronize and queue messages for your action anytime an Internet connection is available and Chrome is running. The best thing about this app is that it is completely free to download and install.

Google Chat (Free)

Google Chat allows you to open your Gmail chat segment in a completely separate window so you can audio, video or text chat with others in your contact list effortlessly. This is the perfect alternative to communicating in real time.

Duolingo (Free)

When you are ready to learn a second (or third!) language, but do not want to shell out the hundreds of dollars some online applications or disc assisted learning options can cost you, Duolingo is a superb option!

Users can choose to study Spanish, French, Italian, German, Portuguese or English directly from their desktop, which helps concentration and a commitment to the process. What's more is that it is completely free!

Spotify (Free)

For some, Spotify is an awesome music streaming source that they have become faithful to, and enjoy a paid subscription that allows listeners to enjoy unlimited music for $9.99 per month. For premium subscribers, the service is available for free without advertisements, and includes free downloads of music.

For those who are more casual online music streamers, with a Facebook account necessary for logging onto the service, up to ten hours of music per month can be enjoyed for free, with advertisements included.

New York Times (Free)

This app is available on Chromebook and absolutely optimized the New York Times for use in the Chrome browser. Tap away at sections of interest and enjoy the exceptional Chrome-page layout that allows you to enjoy the Times in a way you never have before. Although a subscription is necessary to enjoy everything the Times has to offer, readers can receive up to ten articles free per month, and even save them for later reading.

Scratchpad (Free)

Scratchpad allows you to open a completely separate window for note taking, to do lists and even last second plans without moving away from the document or page you are working on. Simply tap the tab and it will appear as a note on top of the current work, web page or email box you are in. You can also save and edit notes quickly and accurately to stay on top of your workload, personal or scholastic life.

Rdio (Free)

Rdio is an online social jukebox, which allows you to enjoy the music you love, while following friends and their musical choices, or those who have similar interests as you to discover new and exciting music, or dredge up some B-side options you didn't know existed.

When you download the app, you will receive a two week trial of advertising free listening that can also be enjoyed offline! Afterwards, if you would like to hang onto your newly found musical prowess, the app is available through Google for $14.99 per month, or $9.99 directly from the Rdio website. There are literally millions of songs available on Rdio, and you can even provide feedback on other's playlists!

Elegant Calculator (Free)

Getting to a calculator on your desktop can wreak havoc on your current workload or social interaction, which is why the Elegant Calculator is so perfect for Chrome. The app is a dropdown calculator that works as a basic version, or a full scientific calculator.

Airdroid

Have an Android phone, such as the Samsung Galaxy lineup? If so, this is the app for you. With Airdroid, you can manage your Android devices such as smartphones and tablets over your Chrome browser. You can use it for moving files such as photos, videos and music, for managing apps, finding your smartphone if it's lost, and even send SMS text messages with it! Airdroid is definitely one to get if you're a loyal Android device owner!

WeVideo

WeVideo is the best way to go in terms of editing videos on your Chromebook. While it's not as advanced as a program you might install on a desktop or laptop computer, it offers the basic video editing features you'll need on Chrome OS. Add this to your device if you might need to make simple edits to any video files you've taken with your webcam, digital camera or smartphone.

WeatherBug (Free)

Want to know what the weather is like for your big holiday weekend? WeatherBug is a beautiful representation of everything unpredictable about Mother Nature, and includes attractive graphs, forecasts, charts and weather maps for your enjoyment, and edification.

Evernote (Free)

Evernote is a brilliant note-taking tool that allows you to sync it across devices. So even though you may have left the grocery list on your Chromebook's desktop, you can access it from your smartphone too, so your trip to the market isn't a guessing game.

Plex

The Plex app for Chrome allows users to stream and share movies, videos and additional media, while it automatically organizes the content for you. No more shuffling around media files, as Plex will provide descriptions, apply artwork and additional helpful information that allows you to find exactly what you are looking for at a moment's notice.

Pixlr Editor

Yet another great photo editor, Pixlr Editor allows you to enhance your photos using basic tweaking options like red eye removal, cropping, resizing, rotating and color and contrast enhancement before you upload the revised image to your social networking sites. You can also access quick colorizing filters, and enjoy a fresh image that reflects all the great things without the picture itself.

Pocket

Pocket is a popular content synching service that uses a browser extension in order to save articles, videos, and pictures online for later offline viewing. The Pocket Chrome App serves as a standalone viewer for all the content that you have saved. With optimized article view, customizable font sizes and backgrounds, tagging, search, archiving, and sharing through email, Twitter, and Facebook available, Pocket provides access to all of the items you find interesting in media, and allows you to view them offline, which is a significant option for those who do not have access to Wi-Fi everywhere.

AudioSauna

Have you ever wanted to make your own music? AudioSauna allows you to start your musical engines in a full audio workstation using this Chrome app. The interface is easy to use, and allows you to create music through a two synthesizers, while accessing samplers and live effects to turn your computer into a DJ booth in no time. You can also enjoy features like ping-pong looping, unlimited layering and key-range mapping.

Mint

Keeping track of your finances may require more than a simple monthly checkbook balancing act. With Mint, you can manage all of your finances, expenditures, budgets and limits in one place. The app will track your credit, bank, loan and retirement accounts for you, categorizing your spending and transactions accurately so you know exactly where your money is going.

Mint can be synced with other devices, and allows you to figure out where to save, how to budget, build financial goals and create bill payment reminders.

Any.do

This app will help to remember everything you have to do on a daily basis. There are millions of Chromebook fans using Any.do to remind them of things to do. It helps to keep all your "to dos" in sync. You will be able to drag and drop in order to plan your agenda. Add reminders so that you will never forget a thing that needs to be done. It gives you the freedom to attach notes and use them as sub-tasks. The best thing is you can view all these tasks while you are offline. You can now try this amazing app for free and derive all the above-mentioned benefits.

Quick Note

The Quick Note app was developed by and in conjunction with Diigo.com. It is the quickest way to take notes in Chrome. This app is especially designed for lightweight note taking. It could be used as a simple notepad, clipboard, to-do list or a scratchpad. You can instantly search for all your notes using this app. It allows for a one-click access to your notes. Quick adding and editing notes are possible in real time. You can also sync your notes with cloud and access them from any part of the world. This is also a free app, which works without an Internet connection.

Planetarium

This free app developed by Neave.Com has an interactive sky map that would help to explore more than 1,500 stars and planets. These stars are considered some of the brightest in the night sky. Most of these starts are visible to the naked eye on a good dark night. You can use this app by clicking and moving your mouse around the sky in order to look for a star. When you point the mouse at a star or planet, it will reveal its name, magnitude, constellation and the distance to our planet in Light Years (LY). This is one great app for folks who are interested in exploring astronomy or teaching it to others such as children.

Solitaire

The Solitaire (Klondike) game is loved by millions of Chromebook users worldwide and most people know the basic rules. The beauty of this particular app is that it can be played with no Internet connection, for those who might be on the road without Wi-Fi access. It is completely free, fast and clutter-free with no ads whatsoever. Add this one if you find yourself on the road a lot with your device and want a game to help pass the time during travel!

Type Fu

This is an app that teaches people to type faster. It will help even a complete beginner to learn typing and improve the speed with time. The app is developed by Type-fu.com and is priced below $5. It works offline and is extremely popular with the users of Chromebook. The app is available for all skill levels and ages. Even a complete beginner, an intermediate or a pro can immensely benefit from this app. It will be fun to learn typing with Type Fu since it includes some engaging exercises. You will never see the same exercise twice with this app. The charts will tell you how much you have improved the typing speed and the accuracy of your typing. It will help you to improve your typing skills even further.

Until AM for Chrome

This app is completely free and accessible without an Internet connection. It is actually a fully-fledged DJ setup squeezed into a lightweight app. It is possible to perform tasks such as adjusting playback speed, modification of sounds through various effects, vinyl scratching with two turntables and do many other things with this app. You are also able to use the music from the cloud while you are online. The possibility of storing thousands of songs in your record base is a salient feature of this app. There are keyboard shortcuts for seasoned users as well. It could be automatically connected to your Google Drive too. Full-screen mode is enabled for undisturbed concentration of the avid music lover.

WorkFlowy

WorkFlowy is another free app, which could be used without an Internet connection on Chromebook. It is a great tool for notes and lists. This app is great for something simple as a shopping list and powerful enough to run a company. It is one of the most flexible note-takers ever designed. The best place to sort and keep track of daily tasks. You can have an infinite amount of nested lists, tag list items, zoom-in on sub lists, expand and collapse lists quickly, mark items as complete and add notes to any list item quite easily. WorkFlowy is really similar to a notepad with superpowers.

World Clocks

This is another free app that could be accessed without an Internet connection. It is actually an interactive digital and analog clock with times shown from more than 400 cities in the world. You can add as many as clocks you want. The drag and drop management of the app helps a great deal in this regard. You can enable 24 or 12h views. Also, the availability of light and dark themes would make it one of the greatest apps to check different times in the world.

As you can see, there are countless apps available already at Google Chrome Web store, and even more will be added in the future. There will also be the ability to use other apps outside of the store in the near future, but for now the 25 Chrome OS apps above should certainly get you on your way with the Chromebook!

Ten Must Have Games for Chromebook

Gaming should never be put on hold, simply because you got a new device. With your Chromebook you can play games in full scale, using the entire screen to enjoy the graphics of your entire favorite gaming outlets.

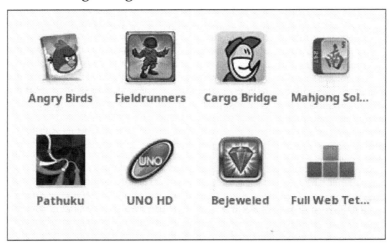

Here are ten that work beautifully with the Chromebook, some of which will also work offline.

Angry Birds (Free)

Yes, yes, and yes: THAT Angry Birds. Chances are you have been playing on a mobile device, using the small screen to eradicate the pigs in your birds' ways. Now, with Chrome, you can use the entire screen to get through the levels effortlessly, while saving your progress in the cloud. There are also Chrome-exclusive levels that make it all worthwhile!

Fieldrunners (Free)

Named as one of Time Magazine's best games of the year, Fieldrunners is a tower defense game where you must build a maze of defensive structures to survive the enemy's attack. With HD Mode and the ability to save your progress in the cloud, you can stop and start whenever you have time for a great gaming session.

Cargo Bridge (Free)

In this fun game players are pitted against physics and geometry, combined with construction capabilities that will test your patience to no end! This puzzle game requires players to use the resources available on screen to build a bridge for their employees to cross. Not strong enough, and the workers will tumble to their demise. The fewer resources you use, the better your score. The full screen helps increase your chances of getting them across, and a leaderboard allows you to keep track of who is the best builder!

Pathuku (Free)

When you are ready to test your skills at the ultimate level, Pathuku is the puzzle game for you. The object of the game is to create the shape provided by only using each line one time. As levels get higher, the shapes you must form become increasingly complicated. The shapes are provided onscreen as a neon outline, and can be incredibly deceptive!

Mahjong Solitaire (Free)

Love solitaire? Love Mahjong? Why not combine the two with this fun, colorful game of skill! Players use the Mahjong tiles instead of cards, requiring matching sets to be clicked and eliminated from the stack to complete the puzzle. The Chrome version mixes it up with multiple stacking layouts and tile variations, and includes a clock to beat so it doesn't seem too much like a walk in the park!

Uno HD (Free)

The old classic Uno is back with the same rules, and the ability to save both your Skip and Draw Two cards to help beat your computerized competitor. You can play against the computer using a time limit to add pressure, while enjoying one of the best color matching games ever released!

Murder Files (Free & Paid)

This classic "Whodunit" style murder mystery game is a fun way to pass the time on your Chromebook. The original free game features an hour-long playable mystery where you attempt to solve puzzles and a mystery during your adventure. There's six episodes in all packed with an English sense of humor. After the first hour-long episode, you'll have the option to pay a bit more to continue playing. Massively entertaining and very addictive, this is a game that crime and mystery game fans will love! (Note: The game is a 366MB download, so keep this in mind when you add it, based on your storage space).

Bejeweled (Free)

Match three or more jewels of the same gem and clear them from the board! Once you have cleared enough jewels in the time allotted, you can move onto the next level. You can also keep track of your friends' scores playing the same game, and post your results to social media to let everyone know who is the boss of this colorful and exciting beat the clock game!

Frogger Classic (Free)

Just like the video game of the 80s, all you have to do is get your frog across the street by dodging traffic. Move the frog up, down, right and left until you have managed to make it across the street, moving onto the next level.

Full Web Tetris (Free)

This fun, but mind-bending game allows you to build block patterns of the same color to remove them from the screen before time runs out. Once you have cleared the screen, you will move onto tougher levels, where the block fragments come raining down at a faster pace.

Although nearly all of the games are free on Chrome, you will most likely have the option to upgrade to a paid version where the advertisements disappear. It is completely up to you whether you want to do so.

How-To, Tips & Tricks

As with any device, there is always a way to get around the system by taking control of the shortcuts available to you. In this case, adding Bluetooth devices, editing images and printing from your browser are all important subjects to understand. Let's get started with some of the most important how-to, tips and tricks for the device.

How to Print

Google Cloud Print is the method used to print documents through the Internet to your printer. You can even use it to print on the road to your home or work printer if it's powered on. However, you'll need to register and connect the printer with your Google account first. Not all printers follow the same instructions, but many of the newer Wi-Fi-ready models of printers, such as the Epson XP-600, may have Google Cloud Print integration built in, making the process easier.

As always, it's important to make sure you aren't going to change around important settings or components if you aren't too familiar with them. You can have someone who knows their technology or an IT professional help with this, or try the instructions provided by Google for your specific printer.

For supported Google Cloud printers and setup instructions: https://www.google.com/cloudprint/learn/printers.html

How to Add Bluetooth Devices

As Chromebook evolves, more and more Bluetooth options will become available. Currently, certain models of the following devices are compatible:

- Headphones
- Headsets (Audio Only)
- Keyboards
- Mice
- Speakers

In order to add them to your Chromebook, first check the lower-right corner of your browser for the Bluetooth symbol. If it appears, your Chromebook is Bluetooth compatible (not all are). Next:

- Click the status area in the lower-right corner, where your account picture appears.
- Select your Bluetooth Status in the Menu.
- Click Enable Bluetooth in the Same Menu. Your Chromebook will automatically begin scanning for available Bluetooth devices.
- Choose the Device you would like to add and Click Connect.

Follow the instructions on the screen to connect your Bluetooth device. These instructions can include adding a PIN for a keyboard, which is randomly generated. If your Bluetooth device is connected, it will be highlighted in the Bluetooth status area menu.

Also, at this time, it doesn't appear that most smartphones and tablets will function over Bluetooth with the Chromebooks. You may find that they will discover each other and connect, but that's about it, as there's no ability to send files via Bluetooth.

Note: If your specific Bluetooth device is not supported it will most likely not show up after a lengthy search.

How to Edit Photos

Chromebook comes with its very own image editor so you can edit pictures before sharing them with the world. To access this easy to use image editor, follow these steps:

- Click on the apps list icon and select Files to open the Files app.
- Select the image you want to edit.
- Click Open at the bottom of the screen.

Once the image is opened onscreen, you can apply any of these edits accordingly:

- Rename: Click on the file name to quickly rename the image. Press Enter to save your changes.
- Mosaic view: When viewing images from Google Drive in the Files app, click the mosaic icon to view your images in a tiled mosaic with large thumbnails. Use the arrow keys to view your images.

- Slide view: Click the slide icon to view your images one at a time on the screen. Use the arrow keys to view your images.
- Slideshow: Click the triangle to view your images in slideshow mode. Use the left and right arrow keys to manually view your images. Press Esc to exit the slideshow or press any key to resume viewing the slideshow automatically.
- Delete: Click the trash icon to delete an image.
- Edit: Click the pencil to see available editing tools at the bottom of the screen. Once you're done with your edits, press Enter to save your edits. If you don't want to save your edit and want to go back to viewing mode instead, press Esc.

Save your images and share them with the people you love, or simply store them in your files for future use.

Extra Storage Options

With Chromebook you already have access to limited storage on the device itself, in addition to the Google Drive. Also consider using USB Jump Drive(s), and/or an External USB drive for storing your files. Keep in mind that not all Chromebooks and jump/flash/external drives may be compatible. More info on file types and external peripherals the Chromebook supports here:

https://support.google.com/chromebook/answer/183093?hl=en

In addition, you can install the free Dropbox app from Chrome Web Store or use Amazon Cloud storage through an Amazon account to store even more files online.

Hooking up Chromebook to a TV

Many Chromebook models include an HDMI output on them. By connecting a HDMI cable to your Chromebook and the other end into a TV or monitor with HDMI input, you can enjoy your display up on the television screen. Use this as a way to watch movies from your Chromebook on the big screen, or to act as a second screen when using your device.

You can also choose to mirror your Chromebook display on the screen as well. You can manage these particular settings by going to Settings>Device and clicking on the "Display" button on your Chromebook.

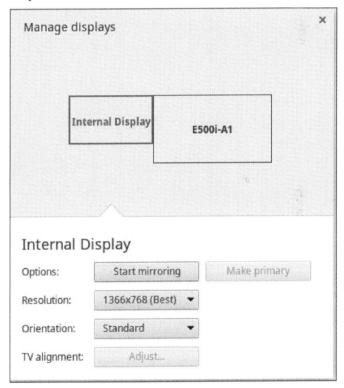

Note: For older televisions or display monitors, it may be possible to use an HDMI output to VGA input adaptor. However, since there are so many distinct models of televisions, and several different models of Chromebooks, it's best to check into this make sure the two will work together properly before buying any additional cables.

How to Use with Chromecast

The Chromecast is a special dongle device created by Google that plugs into your television and allows you to send content (web browser tabs, videos, etc.) from various devices to your TV screen. The Chromebooks generally work great with the Chromecast for streaming browser tabs to a television monitor. Of course, you'll need the Chromecast device, which generally costs $35 or less. You'll also need to install the Chromecast extension for your Chrome browser using a Wi-Fi connection at your home or other location. Once you've got it set up you can begin streaming browser tabs, and using it to watch videos from various sites such as YouTube, Amazon Instant Video, Google Play, and more.

More details on using the Chromecast are available in the guidebook listed at the end of this manual.

Smartphone as Wi-Fi Hotspot

Various models of smartphones that have 3G/4G connectivity may be able to work as a Wi-Fi hotspot for your Chromebook. One tested example is the Samsung Galaxy S5 that was able to provide a wireless Internet connection for the Samsung Chromebook 2. Keep in mind, some smartphones may not link up with all models of Chromebooks, but in general if your current smartphone has this ability, consider using it with your Chromebook when on the road or traveling.

There are also certain wireless providers such as AT&T and Virgin Mobile that offer their own mobile hotspot devices you can purchase. With these wireless modem devices you can use 3G or 4G wireless service on the go, for a fee (usually monthly or a one-time usage fee). Consider this as another option to keep your Chromebook connected when you're on the go. As always, you should first consult with the specific provider to see if the hotspot device will work with your specific brand of Chromebook.

Wired Network Connection

Most Chromebooks will not have an Ethernet input on them as they primarily connect to Wi-Fi (or 3G/4G). However, there are USB to Ethernet adapters you can get to handle that. One end of the adaptor will have a USB cable to plug into your Chromebook. You'll need to plug an Ethernet cable into the slot on the adaptor and then into a network/modem but this should help you get a wired Internet connection.

Note: You may want to check with the specific brand/maker of the USB to Ethernet adaptor first to make sure it will work with your Chromebook before making a purchase.

49

Delete and Caps Lock

Most Chromebooks arrive with a smaller-sized keyboard layout. Many owners of these devices will notice there is a few keys missing that appear on most standard keyboards. The best example is that both the "delete" and "caps lock" keys are absent from a Chromebook's keyboard. However, there are ways to use or add the functionality of both.

Delete

To use the "delete" key hold down the "alt" key and press "backspace." This will delete letter by letter. You can also use ctrl + alt + backspace to delete full words.

Caps lock

For "caps lock" you can press "Alt" + the search key (looks like a magnifying glass). This will turn on CAPS. To turn it off, press "Alt" + the search key again.

You can also change the search key to act as the "caps lock" key. Click on the lower right corner bar where your Google account photo appears, then select "Settings." In the "Device" area click on "Keyboard settings" and then you can use the menu to adjust the behavior of the search key. Click "OK" when finished.

Check Battery Health Status

You can get an indication of the current health status of the battery inside your Chromebook very easily. Simply press ctrl + alt + T keys at the same time. This will open what is known as the Chrome OS Developer shell. At the prompt type in "battery_test 0" (without the quotation marks). You'll receive a quick status report on the battery's current discharge rate and health percentage.

```
Welcome to crosh, the Chrome OS developer shell.

If you got here by mistake, don't panic!  Just close this tab

Type 'help' for a list of commands.

crosh> battery_test 0
Battery is Discharging (65% left)
Battery health: 100%
Please wait..
Battery discharged 0.0% in 0s
crosh>
```

USB Recovery Flash Drive or Disk

You can create your own USB Recovery flash drive for your Chromebook in case of any future issues with the Chrome OS on your device. To do this you will need a 4GB or larger USB jump drive (or SD card). You may also need a Windows PC or MAC computer to downloaded the Recovery files with to your drive.

Note: For the two different methods of creating a recovery drive, you'll need to get your specific Chromebook model code. You can obtain this to write down by pressing and holding down the "esc" (escape) + "refresh" (F3) buttons and then press the power button. You may need to press power again to boot up, but now you will be in developer mode. Your specific model code is at the bottom of the screen. Write this down because you will need it for the two different methods listed below.

First Method to Create Recovery Disk

Owners of M35+ Chromebooks can go to the Google Chrome Web Store and install the Chromebook Recovery Utility for free. Make sure you have your drive or SD card inserted into the Chromebook so you can create the recovery disk. You'll need the Chromebook model number that you obtained earlier to do this.

Second Method to Create a Recovery Disk

1. First, insert the flash drive or SD card into a Windows PC. (You'll be erasing all current data on the drive or card so make sure files are saved elsewhere).

2. Download the Chrome OS Recovery Tool < https://dl.google.com/dl/chromeos/recovery/chrom eosimagecreatorV2.exe> from Google.

3. Once you've downloaded the file, move it to your jump drive or SD card you want to install it on. Next, double-click the file and click either "Yes" or "Run" on the window that pops up for the file.

4. You may receive a security warning at first. Click "Yes" or "Run" again if you do.

5. You'll see a Create Chrome OS Recovery Media dialog box. Type "Parrot" (without the quotes) and you'll see various Chromebook model names listed. Choose the model of your particular Chromebook and click "Next."

6. Choose your USB flash drive or SD card and click "Next."

7. You will be reminded that all files on the flash drive or card will be deleted with this process. Click on "OK."

8. The image will be created on your flash drive or SD card. It could take over 10 minutes for the image to be created. Click "Finish" when the process has completed.

You can now use this drive or disk to reinstall Chrome OS on your Chromebook if you experience any future issues with your device.

How to Factory Reset (Powerwash) Chromebook

There may be some instances where you need to reset a Chromebook to resolve an issue, or if you are giving it to someone else. Keep in mind that following these instructions will delete all data that is stored on the Chromebook including downloaded files, photos, owner permissions, and saved networks. Data you have stored in the cloud, online, or in external drives should not be affected.

Here's how to factory reset or "Powerwash" the Chromebook:

1. Click on the lower right bar on your screen with your Google account photo.

2. Choose "Settings" and then choose "Show advanced settings" at the bottom of that page.

3. In the "Powerwash" section choose "Reset" option.

4. A window will pop up. Choose "Restart."

Note: Another way to reset the Chromebook is to make sure you are signed out of your Google account and then hold down the Ctrl+Alt+Shift+R keys at the same time. Click on "Restart" and wait for the Chromebook to restart. Select "Reset" to complete the process.

After a restart in either of the above methods, you'll receive the original setup screen. You can log into your Google account as the owner of the Chromebook and proceed from there.

How to Play Minecraft on Chromebook

Unfortunately, the popular game Minecraft is not available at the Chrome Web store as a game, and hasn't been developed to run on the Chrome OS. However, that doesn't mean hardcore enthusiasts of the game can't play it.

It will require going through a process of "rooting" your Chromebook so that it can access the Linux kernel (complex terminology for installing a different operating system). It basically changes your Chromebook into more of a traditional laptop, which is discussed in the next tip. The creators of Minecraft, Mojang, have noted that performing the process of rooting on a Chromebook "does not ensure full compatibility" with Minecraft.

Can You Install a Different OS?

Is it possible to hack the Chrome OS, or install a different operating system? The answer to this is "Yes," but more importantly, why would you want to? The Chromebooks were created as a way for people to use a lightweight, portable, quick-booting notebook or laptop that has plenty of functionality through the Chrome OS. The common argument suggests that if you prefer Microsoft Windows OS, or Apple's OS, then it's best to buy these brands of notebooks, although they'll likely be a bit pricier.

While it's not advised to do so, it is possible to install different operating systems on a Chromebook and there are plenty of instructions to be found via Google searches or forums. Windows and Linux are a few operating systems that some people have been able to work with on various Chromebooks.

For example, the site at the link below (not affiliated with this eBook) provides step-by-step instructions to install Linux, Ubuntu and Crouton on a Chromebook:

How to Install Linux on a Chromebook – Lifehacker < http://lifehacker.com/how-to-install-linux-on-a-chromebook-and-unlock-its-ful-509039343/all>

Just keep in mind you may wipe out data on your device if you don't back it up first, and "hacking" could lead to warranty violations of your specific product. Another consideration is that your Chromebook may not have the storage capacity to install another operating system, so keep this is in mind before trying it. If you to decide to go forth with it, make sure you've created a USB flash drive recovery disk per the earlier instructions in this guide first in case of any issues where you need to recover Chrome OS.

Chromebook Troubleshooting

While many Chromebook owners report never having any problems with this device, there are bound to be occasional issues. Below are several common problems across all Chromebook devices with some troubleshooting advice to solve them.

Chromebook Won't Power On

If your Chromebook will not power on, try the following:

- Make sure your Chromebook is charged.
- If that was not the problem, hold down the power button for at least 10 to 20 seconds.

Chromebook Keeps Crashing

If your Chromebook is crashing, it can be incredibly frustrating, and it can make it impossible to get anything done using the device. If your Chromebook keeps crashing try the following options:

- Restart the device.
- If that does not work, turn the Chromebook off for a few minutes, and then turn the power back on.
- Finally, remove the battery for 15 seconds, reinsert the batter, and turn the power on.

Applications Freezing

Sometimes the Chromebook applications freeze. When this happens, try the following:

- Hold the power button down to restart the device.
- If that does not work, do a hard reset by holding down the Power and Refresh buttons.
- Try to log in as a guest and see if the problem persists.
- Try clearing your Domain Name System cache.
    1. Type chrome://net-internals/#dns in the address bar.
    2. Click Clear host cache.

Pages Won't Load

If pages will not load on your Chromebook, you may have an Internet connection issue. To solve a slow or non-existent Internet connection, try the following:

- Start with simply re-enabling Wi-Fi on your Chrome device.
- If that does not work, rebook the Chromebook and then re-enable Wi-Fi.
- For a weak Wi-Fi signal, disable 3G cellular in the drop-down menu at the top of the device's screen. This may solve the issue because 3G can interfere with a weak Wi-Fi
- If none of the options above work, restart your router and modem. While waiting for the router and modem to reset, clear your cache and cookies.
- Tell your Chromebook to "forget" the Wi-Fi network, and then re-add it.
- Make sure your router's network mode is set to BG-Mixed instead of Mixed to improve speed.

If none of steps above work, try the Chromebook Internet Connection Troubleshooter < https://support.google.com/chromebook/troubleshooter/12 57251>.

Why Can't I Install Software

You cannot install Android apps or software intended for Windows operating systems on a Chromebook. Anything you can install on the Chromebook (unless you change your OS or use the Linux instructions above) will be available at the Chrome Web Store. If it does not come from there, you will not be able to install it.

These are just a few general Chromebook troubleshooting steps to take. If you are having any other issue with your Chromebook, check out the Chromebook Known Issues < https://support.google.com/chromebook/known-issues/28748?hl=en> from Google to try to find a solution to your problem.

Ten Great Chromebook Accessories

Many Chromebook models simply include the Chromebook device, power cable/brick, and a few sets of papers such as quick start guides and warranty information. However, there are all sorts of additional accessories you might want to consider adding along with your device to get more from it.

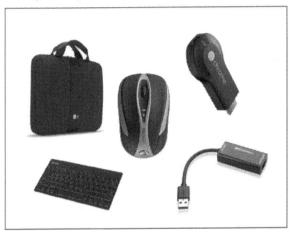

Protective Shell Case & Screen Protector

You may want to get a case & screen protector so you can be sure that your Chromebook won't get damaged if you were to handle it in a rough way. There are various protective plastic cases that can clip on to your particular Chromebook, so that they'll provide protection and also some style or color. iLLumiShield screen protectors are available and very well reviewed if you want to have something that will cover your screen and keep it smudge free.

Carrying Case

A carrying case from a brand such as Case Logic might be perfect for your Chromebook if you're on the go a lot. A case can really make the job of protecting your Chromebook a lot more simple, and also make it easier to transport from location to location. When looking at various carrying cases you might want to consider something with some pockets so you can store extra accessories you need to bring along.

Stereo Headphones

Stereo headphones are a must because most Chromebooks just have a single speaker on them that can't really play anything too loud. Due to this aspect you may want to check into headphones that will allow you to hear the audio more clearly.

Beats by Dre headphones are a top brand if you like higher quality sounds. Bose also makes an excellent lineup of headphones, and there are other less expensive models out there as well from various brand names. These headphones are a must-have accessory for you if you want to enjoy great quality sound while traveling or using the device in quiet areas.

Google Chromecast

The Google Chromecast was previously mentioned in this guide and for a price point of $35 or less, makes a smart buy for those who want to cast their Chromebook screen to a TV monitor.

Simply plug the Chromecast into a TV's HDMI port, install the Chromecast browser extension on your Chromebook, and you're ready to begin streaming webpages, videos, and other content straight to your TV screen!

Cables (HDMI, Audio Out)

There are other cables you can get that can help you hook your Chromebook to a TV or display monitor. An HDMI cable is a great way to stream your Chromebook's display to your TV. Another cable you may want to get if you have an older television would be an adaptor that attaches HDMI to VGA. You'll also find that an audio out cord is a good idea to get so you can hook your Chromebook up to external speakers because not all Bluetooth speakers will function with the device.

Extra Storage (USB Flash & External Drives)

You can use a flash drive to store extra files beyond what your Chromebook allows. These days USB flash (or jump) drives and inexpensive and can hold a lot of additional files. An external USB hard drive is yet another great consideration to really bump up storage capacity. One model that is worth looking at is the SanDisk Connect 64GB Wireless Drive. This will function not only through the USB on many Chromebooks but also as a wireless storage drive.

You can also take a look at the Google page < https://support.google.com/chromebook/answer/183093?hl =en> to see what kind of hard drive you can use with the Chromebook and other file types that are supported.

USB External Webcam

A USB webcam is a great tool to have, especially if you don't like using the version included with your Chromebook or if you don't even have a webcam as part of the model you bought. You can find quality webcams that offer HD images for decent prices online. However, it's always important to consult with the creator of the webcam and your specific Chromebook to ensure they will work together, as some external devices may require installation of drivers.

Bluetooth Mouse & Keyboard

You can use a Bluetooth mouse and/or keyboard if you want to connect to your Chromebook without having to use any wires. They're also perfect for anyone who prefers the efficiency of these items to the keyboard and touchpad their particular Chromebook has.

The iPazzPort Slim Bluetooth Mini Wireless Keyboard is a fantastic option for a keyboard and its small and easy to store. The Bornd C170B Bluetooth wireless mouse is well reviewed and works with your Chromebook as well. The Microsoft Bluetooth 5000 Notebook Mouse is yet another great option that will work with various models of the Chromebook.

USB to Ethernet Adaptor

A USB adapter that helps you hook up to an Ethernet cable connection is a good idea to look into. This is because some people aren't going to have wireless Internet or may not want their connection to be broadcast to others because they're worried about privacy. With a USB to Ethernet adaptor, you'll also want to get an Ethernet cable to plug into the adaptor. This is a great item for travelers to consider in case a hotel only has a wired connection available in the room.

Backup Power Supply/Battery

A backup battery is another good idea to look into. You can find them on some shopping sites and they are generally made by a third party source. Always make sure to read the reviews in case customers have complained. You'll also want to ensure that the specific item works with your Chromebook model. A spare battery is smart to get if you're always using your Chromebook away from home or without an electricity source nearby. Since a battery lasts quite a few hours on a Chromebook, you could probably use it all day without plugging it in with a backup battery.

Conclusion

As you can see from this guide, the Google Chromebook is a useful device that can do quite a bit more than one might think after the first few times it's used. While it is not quite the same as a traditional laptop, it certainly has features and conveniences that tablets and smartphones do not have. The quicker boot-up time, larger screen and keyboard can be a huge asset depending on what you need to do with the Chromebook. In addition, there's no installed software or programs to constantly update, and built-in security that prevents any potential harm to the device.

While it might seem these notebook-style computers can't do much, there's plenty of capability for being productive online. In addition, you can even do some work while offline if you need to. While the Chromebook works the best when connected to the Internet, it still provides enough functions overall to be useful enough offline in terms of entertainment and productivity tasks.

Of course the Chromebook is not for everyone, but if you have one, take some time to learn how to get the most out of it. You will end up really liking these affordable laptop-like devices, and with the addition of newer apps, as well as the potential for Android app compatibility, Chromebooks may just take online computing to the next level!

Additional Resources

Chromebook Buyer's Info & FAQ <
http://amzn.to/1t7gFCV>

Browser Native Chromebook Tips <
http://browsernative.com/tag/chromebook-tips/>

Chromebook Central Forum at Google Groups <
https://groups.google.com/forum/#!category-
topic/chromebook-central/>

Chrome Story Chromebook Tips <
http://www.chromestory.com/google-chromebook/>

PCWorld Chromebook Power Tips <
http://www.pcworld.com/article/2089883/chromebook-
power-tips-how-to-work-smarter-online-and-offline.html>

Generic Chromebook Troubleshooting Infographic <
http://i.imgur.com/BrVVyNi.png>

More Books by Shelby Johnson

Chromecast User Manual: Guide to Stream to Your TV (w/Extra Tips & Tricks!)

Google Nexus 7 User's Manual: Tablet Guide Book with Tips & Tricks!

iPad Mini User's Guide: Simple Tips and Tricks to Unleash the Power of your Tablet!

iPhone 5 (5C & 5S) User's Manual: Tips and Tricks to Unleash the Power of Your Smartphone! (Includes iOS 7)

Kindle Fire HDX & HD User's Guide Book: Unleash the Power of Your Tablet!

Facebook for Beginners: Navigating the Social Network

Kindle Paperwhite User's Manual: Guide to Enjoying your E-reader!

How to Get Rid of Cable TV & Save Money: Watch Digital TV & Live Stream Online Media

Roku User Manual Guide: Private Channels List, Tips & Tricks

Printed in Great Britain
by Amazon